Essential
Delegation
Skills

Carla L Brown

Gower

© 1997 National Press Publications, Inc.
A Division of Rockhurst College Continuing Education
Centre, Inc.

First published in the USA by National Press
Publications Inc.
This edition published by
Gower Publishing Limited
Gower House
Croft Road
Aldershot
Hampshire GU11 3HR
England

British Library Cataloguing in Publication Data

Brown, Carla L.
    Essential delegation skills
    1. Delegation of authority
    I. Title
    658.4'02

ISBN 0 566 0794 45

Typeset in Palatino by Raven Typesetters, Chester
and printed in Great Britain by Biddles Ltd, Guildford.

Contents

1

The big switch: learning to delegate

The surest way for an executive to kill himself is to refuse to learn how, and when, and to whom to delegate work.
J.C. Penney

Knowing how much to delegate is a difficult problem for managers. Somewhere along the way the successful manager learns to switch the focus of activity from doing to planning. There is a direct correlation between management position and the amount of time required in planning and in operating. The allocation of time to managerial functions such as planning is not fixed but varies from industry to industry and from one person to another.

1

Susan and Marge went to work at a local bank directly after leaving school. They entered as clerk/typists. They learned the ropes and worked hard. Each began to advance from clerk to secretary to cashier to account representative. These young women were go-getters. They knew the business better than other clerk/typists. They were good and they knew it. They thrived on challenge and learning. As they moved up their professional ladders, they moved into positions of greater supervisory importance. In the span of a few years each was promoted to senior manager of the bank. No one doubted that Susan was capable. Over the years Susan had acquired a talent for handling the bank's computer programming problems. She worked hard, was thorough and was capable of meeting demands. Yet Marge was obviously star material. Somehow Marge seemed a step ahead of Susan. Susan's staff always delivered their workload in a capable manner, but that was it. They did the job and nothing more. What happened to Susan? Somewhere along the way, Susan was sidetracked. She missed the 'switch'. Because of her history of hard work with the organization, she found it difficult to overcome her superwoman mentality. She was unable to settle for less than what she considered perfect. Susan was a doer, not a delegator. Marge stayed on track and grabbed the 'switch' from doer to delegator.

The higher you advance up the managerial ladder, the less time you should spend doing specific tasks. The higher you advance, the more time you should spend planning and managing. Saxon Tate, managing director of Canada and Dominion Sugar, explains it by saying:

> Decisions simply must be made at the lowest possible level for management at the top to maintain its effectiveness. I make few decisions with a time span of less than a year. At one point I made them for as short a time span as one week. I now see that kind of involvement in detail as a luxury no man at the top can afford.

Robert H. Breckenridge, president and chief executive officer of Vitronics Corporation, one of America's fastest-growing companies, recalls once taking over a new job and being told by his boss 'to make sure you are the least busy of all the people associated with you'. Says Breckenridge, 'By this he meant that I should organize myself and the people who worked for me so that I had the least to do on a day-to-day basis, and could spend time thinking about the actual future of the business.'

An old management axiom observes that 80 per cent of the work is done by 20 per cent of the people. Have you experienced days when you felt that 99 per cent of the work was done by one per cent of the people – namely you? By failing to delegate, you are leading an army of one ... and armies of one go nowhere. A great coach doesn't don the boots and shinpads and take the field to mask and tackle. He concentrates on strategy and tactics. The most effective managers are more concept-oriented than task-oriented.

Planning is exerting control over the future. You cannot control the future if you are trapped in the present. For those trapped in the present, a key to the future is delegation. Delegation is assigning to others specific tasks and the requisite authority to complete those tasks, with mutually agreed methods for evaluating the completed work. The primary reason that managers fail is the inability to delegate properly. Delegation is a leveraging technique. The successful delegator can double or triple his or her productivity. The non-delegator works frantically, grabs lunches, lugs briefcases, is subjective and generally ineffective. The delegator has time for work and personal life, works effectively and views life objectively. The advantages of delegation for you are quite simple – you are using other people's brains for your gains. As the axiom goes, you learn to work smarter, not harder.

The choice is yours. Are you ready to make the switch?

Are you doing the right job?

How well do you delegate? Are you doing the right job? Could improved delegation make your job more interesting and easier? Many quizzes have been devised to give managers a reading on how they rate as a delegator. The following checklist is representative of most. If your answer is yes to none or only one of the 20 questions, you are doing well as a delegator. If you answer yes to four or more of the questions, there is room for improvement in your delegation skills.

1. Are you a perfectionist? Are you proud of it?

2. Do you take work home regularly?

3. Do you work longer hours than your subordinates?

4. Do you spend too much time doing for others?

5. Do you often wish that you could spend more time with your family?

6. When you return to the office, is your in tray too full?

7. Do you still keep a hand in the job you held before your last promotion?

8. Are you often interrupted with queries or requests?

9. Can you name immediately your top three work goals?

10. Do you spend time on routine details which others could handle?

11. Do you like to keep a finger in every pie?

12. Do you rush to meet deadlines?

13. Are you unable to keep on top of priorities?

14. Do you frequently feel overworked?

15. Is it hard for you to accept ideas offered by others?

16.   Do you attract followers rather than leaders?

17.   Do you give over-detailed instructions to subordinates?

18.   Do you believe higher-level managers should work more?

19.   Do you hold daily staff meetings?

20.   Do you worry that your employees will show you up?

A top investment banker recently attended a time management seminar. Accurately assessing his delegation problems, he returned to the office determined to make changes. He and his secretary listed every item that had crossed his desk in the last week – phone calls, memos, requests for reports, etc. He noted the relative importance of every item, whether it could have been delegated and, if so, to whom. He then directed all assignable tasks to the appropriate persons with instructions 'to handle the tasks'.

This executive described the reaction as follows:

> Some dust was stirred up. There were a lot of discussions, but almost every single delegated task was effectively handled. Many of them were taken care of far better than if I had done them. This changed my whole outlook on the job and has made me far more effective.

2

Stop that thief! The advantages of delegation

There are people who want to be everywhere at once and they seem to get nowhere.
Carl Sandburg

Poor delegation means poor management. Good delegation is the cornerstone of good management skills. Ineffective delegation hinders the success of an entire office. Allowing poor delegation skills to continue steals the sense of satisfaction in a well-run workplace. Ineffective delegation drains energy right out of the workplace. Lack of delegation also holds families hostage to the never-ending workloads. Start delegating – stop stealing.

Stealing from your subordinates

Failure or refusal to delegate robs subordinates of initiative and job satisfaction. Chaos reigns. When methods become more important than results, the operation stagnates. No one has the power to decide or communicate. Everyone waits on the word from 'upstairs'. Rote work becomes easier the more it is repeated. Workers memorize their jobs like actors learn lines for a play. Boredom sets in.

A large carpet store reached a point where a full-time assistant manager was required. The owner interviewed and hired a capable young business graduate from a local university. The assistant studied hard, kept busy and was a great help. After 18 months, the assistant gave notice and went to work for a competitive chain of retail stores. Why? The assistant had been busy but not responsible. The owner had failed truly to delegate. Delegation involves responsibility and authority, not just busy work. Delegate, don't dump. Delegation must challenge the worker to grow and expand their horizons.

Stealing from the company

When the £25-an-hour manager does a £10-an-hour job, the company is shortchanged £15 right away. Actually, the company is losing more than £15. Companies lose the chance for productivity growth. If you spend a half-hour delegating and your subordinate spends four hours working on the task, you have effectively created up to eight times the results you would have had had you not delegated.

An associate came to the office of young Missouri Senator Harry Truman seeking a specific report. Truman's secretary was at lunch. Rather than tell the person that his secretary would find the document when she returned, Truman spent 30 minutes of his time looking for it. Only a few months later, he became President and had to shift into high gear. No longer could he waste time performing tasks someone else could and should easily do.

Stealing from yourself

Ineffective delegation undermines the professional and personal lives of everyone. By delegating details, managers become specialists in the art of managing. They are not trapped by excelling at one task. They can walk into any division of a company prepared to make it function. They know people and how to develop them. They use people power to do the unique tasks of the department while they manage.

One successful delegator relates the story of the proficient cocktail server who was willing to accept the challenge of his delegation. Within 36 months this young woman moved up from serving cocktails to being a restaurant manager. She became a key member of the management team in a £12 million business.

Stealing from your family

Ineffective delegation skills will also cramp your personal life. Do you stay late, take work home, feel that you are the only one who can handle the job? We all know people who live their jobs. They work late, rush lunches, lug work home and never take a holiday. These people fear a loss of control when they delegate. The effective manager doesn't need to know how a word processor works. He must understand what it does and how to delegate tasks to those who do understand how it works.

John, carrying two briefcases, always arrived late for dinner. One night his five-year-old daughter asked Mummy why Daddy had to carry two suitcases everywhere. Mummy proudly explained that Daddy was an executive with lots and lots of work to do. More work than he had time to do at the office. The child spoke to the heart of the matter: 'Why don't they just put him in a slower group?' John had failed to switch from being a doer to a delegator.

3

Barriers to delegation

It is often safer to be in chains than to be free. Franz Kafka

Delegation involves chance. Chance is risky. It is a question of control. When a job is delegated, there are feelings attached to the transfer of responsibility: loss of power, loss of authority, loss of achievement, etc. Even though some of these feelings are uncomfortable at times, the risk is worth it when you consider the benefits of delegation. These emotions aren't negative, but they do hinder effective delegation. Examining these barriers will help you develop your 'delegation consciousness'.

Barriers in the manager

I can do it better

This fallacy of omnipotence is often found among managers. Even if the manager can do a better job, the choice is not between the quality of his or her work and the quality of the subordinate's; it is, rather, between the benefits of the manager's better performance on a single task and the benefits derived when he or she devotes that time to planning, delegating, supervising, and training and developing a team. Eventually such a team will both outperform and outlast the manager.

Lack of confidence in subordinates

This is a never-ending cycle. When delegation is withheld because of lack of confidence, subordinates are denied the opportunity to develop the very abilities they need to warrant confidence. This makes the manager's doubts a self-fulfilling prophecy.

Insecurity

Do not be afraid of being disliked by subordinates. Delegation is not tyranny. Don't be afraid to ask others to increase their job responsibilities. Also, don't be afraid you will appear to be dispensable to the company. Delegation is a management tool designed to help you get greater results with less effort. Hectic pace is not a sign of achievement, but of inefficiency.

Barriers in the

14   Essential Delegation Skills

your boss and co...
of your di...
nate...

Lack of experience/co...

Your subordinates may no...
tasks that you want to assign to...
skills and experience. Perhaps the...
to make changes; replace those wh...
Another way to solve the problem is ...
tion as a form of coaching. Begin with ...   ...n-
ment of simple, routine tasks. Step by step, ...elop
each subordinate's level of skill and competence. It
takes great patience, but it can be done.

Avoidance of responsibility

Go slowly. Clarify your ideas of delegation as you
extend the scope of your delegating. As subordinates
see the advantages they gain in the process, their
resistance will vanish. Fashioning a series of small
successes is the best way to handle these cases. Each
delegation should help the employee build up confidence for the next one.

Barriers in the situation

Lack of organization

When your boss assigns a task to one of your subordinates without telling you, chaos is the immediate
result. You can no longer effectively delegate to that
subordinate. What you must do is sit down with

me to some mutual understanding ties and those of each of your subordi- s. Discuss the company's or department's organization chart. Explain the confusion that results when he or she shoots from the hip in handing out assignments.

Staffing problems

Having an insufficient staff of overworked subordinates can be a big stumbling block when seeking to delegate. But it's not an impossible situation. Do whatever you must do in an effort to hire additional people. This can mean taking on an additional staff member or two, or hiring specialists from the outside. If you're not able to add people, check the subordinates you do have. Are they using their time efficiently? Are they delegating to their subordinates? In most cases you shouldn't worry about the situation; delegate anyway. You're almost sure to find that your subordinates are flexible enough to handle the additional work.

4

What to delegate

What is worth doing is worth the trouble of asking somebody to do it.
Ambrose Bierce

'A good staff will find the work to do.' Ridiculous. Why should the staff 'find' work to do? That's your job now – managing and directing work. Why invent jobs or stretch out work to placate a boss who says things like 'I don't want to see anybody sitting around with nothing to do'. Even though people sometimes slide through their workday, there's no reason you should choose inefficient and often directionless management.

If you're blessed with a legion of self-starters, you're lucky. However, in general, unless you think of yourself as the main source of new work for your staff, few new things will be done. Encouraging the 'busy look' merely ensures old tasks will be done with increasingly less efficiency. Every manager should strive to make themself dispensable to the operation of their company. Successful delegation develops the maximum potential of your team to such a point. As a manager, the important thing is not what happens when you are there, but what happens when you are not there. The very drive and determination that earmark successful workers are often the same qualities which hinder effective delegation. Outperforming a subordinate on a specific task is not the issue. The choice is a comparative advantage between managerial success on one specific task and the successful coaching, planning and directing (managing) of an entire team.

Since your own work forms the main source of responsibilities to be delegated, making a detailed list of the jobs you do is crucial. The key word is 'detailed'. Unfortunately, most work does not fall neatly into specific categories of delegation. How, then, do you decide what to delegate and what not to delegate? The following guidelines might help you decide.

Delegate the routine and the necessary

These are the jobs that you have done over and over. These are often the necessary tasks of the job that are routinely dictated by your company. You know them. You know the problems, the unique peculiarities, the specifics of how to do these jobs. These are the easiest jobs to delegate. Because you know these tasks so well, you can easily explain and delegate them away.

Are you required to attend regularly scheduled informational meetings that could easily be handled by your subordinates? For the past several years a senior manager in a local bank was required to attend a monthly council luncheon of all financial institutions in the community. These luncheons were primarily social and rarely yielded anything that could not have been handled by the manager's assistant. The manager realized that this was a doing job, not a planning job. He called in his assistant and explained the function of this meeting. The young assistant was eager and enthusiastic for a chance to meet her colleagues in a professional setting. This was the perfect opportunity for successful delegation.

Delegate the specialist tasks

Would you perform surgery on your family? Probably not, unless you happen to be a surgeon. Would you represent yourself in court without a lawyer? Probably not, unless you happen to be a lawyer. You would look for the most skilled person in the field. The same is true in the office. Take advantage of any specialist skills that exist in your office. If you are responsible for choosing a new word-processing system, you could do the research yourself – or you could delegate the initial research to the computer

programmer in your office. If you have a maths whiz in the office, that person could assume the responsibility of double-checking the maths in all the reports.

Beware of the superman syndrome. Realize that there are occasions which require delegation of tasks you normally perform to skilled professionals such as lawyers, accountants and temporary overload staff. At such times, make sure to check references for the best possible person. Don't just reach for the phone directory. Match your need to the skills of the people available to you. Practice selective/discriminating delegation here.

Delegate 'occupational hobbies'

These are the duties you should have delegated a long time ago, but haven't because they're too much fun. It's okay to keep a couple, but at least recognize them for what they are: easy and enjoyable ... and much better done by somebody else. It may seem paradoxical to delegate the very aspects of your job that you enjoy most. Yet these are often the tasks that you hang on to even though they don't represent the best use of your time and energy. They are often related to your area of expertise or earlier positions that you have had with the company. This has been referred to as 'turf mentality' – holding on to specific duties becomes a manager's means of protecting his turf.

A sales manager has been attending the same international trade show each year for several years. She looks on the assignment as a chance to get away and see old friends. Actually, it's no longer necessary for the sales manager to be there. One of her sales representatives could achieve the same results. Do you see yourself in this or comparable situations? Are you simply indulging yourself? Wouldn't your career be better served by spending the time at your desk? Take a look at your priorities.

5

What not to delegate

The buck stops with the guy who signs the cheques.
Rupert Murdoch

While the majority of managers err on the side of not delegating enough of their workload, there is the occasional manager who delegates far too much. For many reasons there are certain tasks that simply cannot be delegated to your subordinates. Executives from managing directors down do have obligations and responsibilities which are not to be delegated. These are among the very reasons that you have your job rather than a subordinate position.

The following are guidelines for determining
what should not be delegated.

Don't delegate rituals

There are certain functions that require a person of
specific position to be present. When a local church
applied for planning permission, the congregation's
solicitor could have represented them at the hearing.
However, in a town where most people knew each
other, the minister realized that his presence at the
meeting – in addition to the lawyer's – would be
important. His presence signified the importance of
this building to the church and the community.

As another example, retiring employees don't
expect to have their retirement gifts presented by the
chairman's secretary. They expect and deserve to
have someone as important as the chairman in attendance.

Don't delegate personnel/confidential matters

Personnel decisions (evaluation, promotion or dis-
missal) are generally sensitive and often difficult to
make. While you may need the confidential input of
your subordinates on personnel issues, the job and
responsibility is yours.

While an analysis of your department's job classi-
fications and pay scales may seem time consuming
and a prime job for delegation, this is a job for management. Imagine the problems in maintaining the
confidentiality of all salaries within a department.
This is not a job to delegate to your subordinates.

Don't delegate policy making

Responsibilities and tasks within a certain policy area can be delegated, but never delegate the actual formulation of a policy. Policy sets the limits of decision making.

Responsibility for policy making within specified, limited guidelines may take place. General credit policies of businesses are developed by credit managers. Yet the ability to grant credit to specific customers up to certain limits is often granted to salesmen.

Don't delegate crises

Crises will inevitably happen. A crisis does not offer the time for initiating delegation. When one does occur, it is the responsibility of the manager to shoulder the problem and find the solution. Studies have shown that in time of crisis and heavy workloads, successful delegators are able to maintain their leadership roles. This is because they have laid the groundwork for delegation prior to the onset of the crisis. Their subordinates are self-motivated and enthusiastic team players. They know what to expect. They are part of a trained team. A crisis in business demands skill and experience.

The manager of a plumbing contracting company discovered that a major client urgently needed cost projections from the company before construction bids for a multi-million pound project could be submitted. The computers for the local contractor's supplier were down that day. The manager faced a crisis as the one who had to make decisions, deal with the general building contractor, determine the availability of parts for other suppliers, etc.

When the heat is on, make sure that you are there to take the lead.

6

Planning what to delegate

There is nothing so useless as doing efficiently that which should not be done at all.
Peter Drucker

Knowing that you need to delegate is easy. Unless you plan to work yourself to death for the glory of the company, you will be happy to give away some of your jobs. What jobs? How do you decide?

Since your job responsibilities are the wellspring of work for your subordinates, you must analyse your job. Are there tasks which initially helped you learn to do the job? Are there jobs which others need to know in order to keep the unit functioning when you're gone? These are definitely jobs that you can successfully delegate to your subordinates. By delegating, you keep yourself growing. You keep your people growing, too. Just because you're bored with a task doesn't mean it couldn't be a wonderful challenge for someone else.

There are eight simple steps that will help you to decide which jobs to delegate:

1.   List all the jobs (results and their subtasks) which you are responsible for.

2.   Keep a separate running list for two weeks of all you do during the day. (Include everything, even answering the phone during lunch breaks.)

3.   List a time estimate for each task.

4.   Review your personnel and their skills and attributes.

5.   Place the name of a staff member by each task, matching skills and attributes with the needs of each task.

6.   Make a list of all the details and instructions an employee will need to accomplish each task.

7.   Decide on checks and balances (evaluation controls) for each task.

8.   Determine alternative time plans for each task (in case the job needs to be redone or is not finished on time).

Having analysed and assessed your work, the next step is to analyse and assess the capabilities of your subordinates. It is essential to present subordinates with challenges which fit their next level of growth. An underchallenged person will quickly become bored. Overchallenge and you'll have a very frustrated, unhappy employee. Mastering this is more an art than a science, but there is one easy way of improving your accuracy. Look at your people. Who's been hinting for more challenge? Open your mind to people who may not seem qualified – often an ounce of enthusiasm is worth a pound of experience. Creative delegation sends a good signal that people in your organization can shape their own futures.

The following checklist can help you decide what kind of project to delegate to a particular subordinate. Does he or she:

- work quickly or slowly?

- seek out new assignments?

- require minimal or maximum direction?

- make a lot of mistakes or only a few mistakes?

- write well or poorly?

- work in an organized or disorganized way?

- like working alone or with others?

- prefer structured work or the opportunity for creativity?

- give strong verbal presentations?

- handle large assignments well?

This analysis is not something to use to make decisions about pay rises, promotions and transfers. Unless you supervise an assembly line, you have a sufficient variety of tasks to interest anyone. Some tasks require speed, others don't. Some require good oral presentation skills, others can be performed without a word being spoken. Some projects require careful thought and analysis, others are simple and straightforward.

Even employees who resist new assignments can and should be delegated to them. It's your responsibility to define tasks which fall within the scope of the person's existing abilities and will reasonably stretch those skills in the training process. So, we come right back to the foundation of delegation: your ability to define jobs and creatively match those jobs to your staff.

7

Effective goal setting in the delegation process

You've got to be very careful if you don't know where you are going,
because you might not get there.
Yogi Berra

The common injunction to 'do your best' is virtually useless in motivating people. Actually, if we think about it, this finding is not surprising at all. Ambiguity is the antithesis of productivity. What does 'do your best' mean? To the worker faced daily with countless variables and demands, it means dozens of things – and because the worker hears it all the time, it comes to mean nothing at all.

Goals must be specific, clearly stated and clearly

measurable. Goals in any endeavour must be specific and few in number. Build tests into each goal to measure the progress made. Goals with these characteristics provide a source of feedback, accountability and evaluation. Well-stated, measurable objectives are invaluable in motivating people and improving their performance. If an employee does not have a clear idea of the task at hand and does not receive feedback on the performance of it, they cannot realistically be accountable for the task. Nevertheless, the chaotic workplace, where no one really knows what to do and seldom gets feedback on what is or is not being done effectively, is more the rule in business.

Goals must be measurable in order to be any good. It's also worthwhile to remember that people understand and respond to quantity more than quality. If you must choose between them while you're defining your goals, go for 'more' rather than 'better'.

Let's be even more concrete. Sound objectives have three identifiable elements:

1. an action verb (to increase, to contact, to sell, to enrol, etc.);

2. a measurable result (five, 50 per cent, 3,000, etc.);

3. the date by which the objective will be accomplished (e.g. 3 p.m. on June 16).

In the beginning, set your goals for a 'marginal' employee with one view in mind: to build successes. Even though the employee will eventually perform at a higher level, don't expect immediate results.

Aim for just a little bit more work than the employee has been doing, aim for what they might succeed in reaching. Success builds on success. If you want a successful performer to do more, don't be afraid to aim high.

A time element is crucial to commitments. Ask and agree on a time for completion. Do not say, 'I want you to get your work done soon'. Instead say, 'The goal is to increase production 10 per cent by 16 June'. And whatever you do, avoid saying, 'Why don't we get together sometime soon and discuss this again'. Rather, say, 'Let's get together on 3 March at 3 o'clock for a review of our progress'. Establish with your employee the understanding that commitments can be renegotiated, but don't be open-ended about it. Getting a firm commitment takes time on your part, but it is an essential element in good supervision.

Without commitment to make them succeed, the best-laid goals are often doomed to failure. It is crucial, therefore, to get your employees committed to the goals. Too often we take commitment for granted and overlook this simple step. You want more than nodded approval or tacit acceptance. Go for an outright statement that the person agrees on the goals and the deadlines. Be prepared to include employee suggestions or modifications in your goals and deadlines. Be flexible. If you have spent considerable time working out a plan in some detail, it makes sense to spend a few more minutes to secure a commitment from your employee that they will put the plan into action.

Even when a plan seems quite workable, you

might want to get a written commitment. Many management experts suggest that each goal and its instrument of evaluation should be written out on paper. Each goal and its evaluation measures should take no more than 250 words, or one side of one piece of paper. Place the accountability where it belongs. Train yourself and your subordinates to review these written goals on a regular basis.

8

Three keys to choosing a delegatee

No duty the Executive had to perform was so trying as to put the right man in the right place.
Thomas Jefferson

Consider this scenario:

Jim, you've been a medical supply salesman for our company for the past five years. You've done such a good job as a salesman – perfect attendance, punctuality, excellent customer relations skills and knowledge of pharmaceuticals – that we want you to come in next week and be a doctor. So here are the keys to Operating Room 9. Feel free to move in. Now don't worry about a thing. We have confidence in you and we'll be there all the way to back you up. Just put on this new stethoscope and pick out some supplies for this medical bag. Get a good feel for the job and get to know the nursing staff.

If this is the job for you, we'll enrol you in a correspondence course offered through the local college. It's called 'The Theoretical Practice of Medicine'. You'll study medical history, human anatomy and how to write like a doctor. After three years we'll teach you how to operate on people.

Thankfully, doctors and surgeons aren't trained this way. Yet similar scenarios are played out daily in the business world. Authority is granted to employees precisely because they are so good at their non-authority jobs. They are terrific, so promote them. But too often the boss forgets to teach them how to do the job.

In many hospitals, for instance, nurses are promoted to department heads with next-to-no training. They are told one day, 'You're the boss'. The next day they have a cluttered office and must figure out what they're supposed to do. Think of the excellent sales people who have been promoted to sales management and were left to sink or swim.

Selection of delegatees has three general goals. In choosing the right delegatee, weigh these goals to determine which are the most important to the task at hand. It's a decision similar to that of selecting a deputy prime minister. The person selected must be competent. However, the candidate must also consider such diverse factors as patching up rivalries within the party and appealing to a wide cross-section of voters.

Direct results

For most cases of delegation, the direct result is the most important goal. (But keep in mind the two other important goals of delegation.)

Mr Addison of Acme Supply has called demanding to know where his 600 cases of widgets are. If the missing widgets are not accounted for within 24 hours, he's threatening to cancel the order. Both Sharon and Sam are capable of tracking the missing widgets. However, Sharon has more experience at tracking diverted orders, and she has dealt directly with Mr Addison and his secretary in the past. So even though Sam could do the job, you opt for Sharon this time. She is obviously more proficient and suited to this particular delegation opportunity.

Development

Development of employee skills always represents an important delegation goal. It also complicates the selection of the delegate. You want the right person, not necessarily the most competent person. Surprisingly, there are numerous opportunities to delegate tasks where the goal of developing the delegatee's skills is paramount and the direct result is of lesser consequence. People, normally half-dead from boredom or frustration during office hours, come alive when given a new challenge and their abilities take a quantum leap. It's far better to have champions working for you than zombies.

Realizing that Mr Addison of Acme Supply is an important customer, you know that your entire staff must handle his account with proper concern and respect. From the first day that Sam joins your staff as an accounting clerk/typist, you begin to explain the importance of the Acme account. Even though Sharon can handle these routine transactions of billing, shipping and accounting for the Acme orders (she's done it for years), you begin to delegate the Acme transactions to Sam. Eventually Mr Addison will call with a rush order or a temper tantrum, as he is prone to do. When the crisis comes, Sam will be ready to respond because you have developed his skills slowly but surely.

Evaluation

Sooner or later subordinates will have to be tested under fire. In some delegations, your main goal is to observe individual performance in a given situation. Be careful not to delegate with the expectation of failure. To do so would eventually reflect unfavourably on you. Delegation does provide indications of employees' strengths and weaknesses which would not otherwise be apparent to managers.

The Director of a food wholesaler needed to fill an account representative's position. He asked his secretary to assist an experienced account manager with a presentation to a brand new supermarket chain. While the job was accomplished in an acceptable manner, the secretary realized that this job was not for her. The working conditions, travel, hours and other things were not what she wanted in a job. Both parties were able to make some important long-term assessments based on this delegation.

Delegation is a useful tool in determining the future potential of employees in the workforce. It is mutually beneficial in allowing the employee to explore all facets of the work done in your business.

In the classic ten-item exercise (see Exercise 8.1) (the results of which have remained consistent in many management training seminars) psychologists have found the results shown in Table 8.1.

Exercise 8.1   Motivation self-assessment worksheet

Rate the most important item 1, the second most important 2
and so on, for each column

	What do subordinates want?	What you want
Interesting work	_____	_____
Job security	_____	_____
Full appreciation of work done	_____	_____
Personal loyalty of manager	_____	_____
High salary or wages	_____	_____
Tactful discipline	_____	_____
Feeling of being 'in on things'	_____	_____
Promotion in the company	_____	_____
Good working conditions	_____	_____
Help with personal problems	_____	_____

Table 8.1   Exercise review: what workers want

	How subordinates rated these items	How managers think subordinates rated them
Full appreciation of work done	1	8
Feeling of being 'in on things'	2	10
Help with personal problems	3	9
Job security	4	2
High salary or wages	5	1
Interesting work	6	5
Promotion in the company	7	3
Personal loyalty of manager	8	6
Good working conditions	9	4
Tactful discipline	10	7

9

Developing people power through delegation

You see, really and truly, apart from the things anyone can pick up (the dressing and the proper way of speaking and so on) the difference between a lady and a flower girl is not how she behaves, but how she's treated. I shall always be a flower girl to Professor Higgins, because he always treats me as a flower girl and always will, but I know I can be a lady to you, because you always treat me as a lady and always will.
Eliza Doolittle in George
Bernard Shaw's *Pygmalion*

Like Professor Higgins, most managers unintentionally treat their subordinates in a way that leads to less-than-desirable performance. The way managers treat their subordinates is subtly influenced by what

41

they expect of them. If a manager's expectations are high, productivity is likely to be high. If their expectations are low, productivity is likely to be low. It is as though there is a law that causes a subordinate's performance to rise or fall to meet the manager's expectations.

J. Sterling Livingston of the Harvard Business School describes the 'Pygmalion in Management Effect' this way:

1. What a manager expects of a subordinate and how he treats the subordinate will combine to profoundly influence the subordinate's performance and his career progress. What is critical in the communication of expectations is not what the boss says, but what he does. Indifference and noncommittal treatment communicates low expectations and leads to inferior performance. Most managers are more effective in communicating low expectations to their subordinates than in communicating high expectations to them, even though most managers believe exactly the opposite.

2. Superior managers create high performance expectations that subordinates can fulfil. Subordinates will not strive for high productivity unless they consider the boss's high expectations realistic and achievable. If they are pushed to strive for unattainable goals, they eventually give up trying. Frustrated, they settle for results that are lower than they

are capable of achieving. The experience of a large electrical printing company demonstrates this. The company discovered that production actually declined if production quotas were set too high because the workers simply stopped trying to meet them. 'Dangling the carrot just beyond the donkey's reach' is not a good motivational device.

3. Less effective managers fail to develop high expectations for their subordinates. Successful managers have greater confidence than ineffective managers in their ability to develop the talents of subordinates. The successful manager's record of achievement and self-confidence grants credibility to his goals. Thus, subordinates accept his expectations as realistic and try hard to achieve them.

Integral to the success of delegation is the development of employees' self-esteem. The availability of self-esteem as a motivator is a recent phenomenon. In the 1930s, the issue was irrelevant. Back then the issues were money, security and survival – the very things that were in short supply. Recent distinct improvements in the satisfaction of these survival needs have brought with them a whole new set of drives. Workers have recently begun to complain about a lack of dignity and respect. With increasing turnover rates, absenteeism and other forms of alienation and dissatisfaction, managers can no longer maintain that all workers care about is a payslip. The fact is, management experts and psychologists have shown that a salary increase is not necessarily the ultimate motivator. Unless you cannot live on your present salary, more money is often a weak incentive. In addition to providing money to live on, most people work every day to satisfy their need for structure and predictability in their lives. Look at the endless number of rich men who continue to work every day. Precisely because their basic needs are being met, today's workers do not automatically accept authoritarian, dehumanizing styles of management. Look at the advancement of the Japanese work styles to the forefront of the business and industry world. Japanese industry has answered the complete needs of the worker as a person, and the success is evident. Workers' priorities have changed. Statistics show that such benefits as interesting work, sufficient help, equipment and information to get the job done, and enough authority/independence to do the job are as important to workers as good pay. None of these newly demanded features is a tangible economic benefit. Rather, each of them is either a subtle or direct result of the need for self-esteem.

In the 1950s, Dr Abraham Maslow defined and listed a hierarchy of human needs. It helps explain why people are motivated to act. Generally, people progress up the hierarchy. However, it is common to find an individual at varying levels in different areas of their life at any given time. Observing employees' needs will help you understand their self-esteem needs. Developing employees' self-esteem is vital to developing the delegating habit.

Maslow listed needs in this order, from most basic to complex:

1. bodily needs (food and shelter);

2. safety (lack of danger);

3. belonging (being part of a group);

4. esteem (status and achievement);

5. self-actualization (insight into one's self-growth).

Managers tend to think the lower needs are more important to their employees. Wages and job security fall into the category of bodily needs. In reality, workers say that being in on things and a sense of appreciation (esteem, belonging and self-actualization) are the most important to them. As a delegator, consider the needs of your staff members with regard to their motivation to accept your delegation. Maslow's research is useful in presenting the delegation request. Consider the vast difference in these two requests:

1. 'The Board of Directors has ordered another regional collection analysis. I'm sorry, but you'll have to contact each county chairperson to collect their totals and compile the various regional totals ... by tomorrow.'

2. 'The Board is really enthused about the campaign totals to date. They are really interested in analysing our progress by region. We need to have updated regional totals to distribute at the meeting tomorrow.'

The first delegation request motivates but does so only through fear of reprimand with an implied sense of failure. The second request accomplishes motivation with an appeal to a sense of accomplishment and belonging to the group.

A thoughtful analysis of employee motivation and work style will greatly assist you in successfully delegating.

Ways to enhance self-esteem

1. Actively listen.

2. Write down others' ideas.

3. Accept others' opinions.

4. Take ideas seriously.

5. Accept differences in others.

6. Give tangible rewards.

7. Give the OK signal when you agree with others.

8. Praise the specific task.

9. Say, 'You are right'.

10. Support others' actions.

11. Recognize feelings.

12. Give special assignments.

13. Ask for help.

10

The delegation meeting

It is never a sign of weakness when a man in a high position delegates authority; on the contrary, it is a sign of his strength and of his capacity to deserve greatness.
Walter Lippman

Don't delegate on the run. A corridor or noisy meeting is not the place to pass along the information required for an important delegation. Schedule sufficient time (without interruption) in your office for the delegation meeting. You may want to allow 10 per cent more time than your initial estimate. This will allow adequate time for discussion and questions.

The first step in delegation is pre-planning on your part. You must give some thought to the delegation process prior to the actual conference. Know what supplies, resources and authority will be needed to do the work. Anticipate what questions or problems the employee might have. Commit to paper your goals for the work. Once you are ready for the delegation meeting, it is helpful to remember the specific steps in the act of delegating work to someone.

The steps in the delegation process

State the desired results

Explain the results that you want the person to achieve. Don't start with the actual tasks required to do the work. Start with the results you want achieved. Don't stress methods over results. You may be surprised at your employee's creativity in devising ways to achieve the desired results. The goal is mutual agreement on an objective achievement.

Consider the difference in these two delegations:

1. 'Katie, make 100 copies of these personnel changes on company letterhead and send one to every store manager. Get on it right away.'

2. 'Katie, there are 100 store managers in the chain and I need to let all of them know about

these personnel changes as soon as possible. I'd like you to handle it. Would you give it some thought and discuss it with me in half an hour?'

Katie may surprise you by suggesting inclusion of the memo in the avidly read company newsletter, which is about to go to press. Or she may say that the only way to do it is to send out 100 form letters. She may also surprise you by not having the vaguest idea of what to do. Great! You now have the chance to teach Katie two things: (1) that there are several ways to disseminate information to 100 people and (2) that you rely on her ideas as well as her help and will continue to ask for both as you delegate.

Having mutually agreed on the goals of the project, commit the revised goals to paper. Remember, clearly state the goal of a project and the performance standard that will measure it in 250 words or less – one sheet of paper. If it takes longer than this, then rethink the delegation and break it down into smaller, more specific functions. Train your subordinates and yourself to review these goals. The only problems in delegation occur when there is a difference between what you want to happen and what is actually happening. Reviewing the mutually agreed goals will avoid this. It minimizes confusion on all parts.

Establish a timeline

If the delegatee has a problem with your suggested deadline, be flexible when possible and work out a more suitable time limit. Allowing the subordinate to set his own deadline is far preferable to forcing yours on him. However, circumstances may sometimes dictate this. Be certain that you clearly prioritize your delegation to the employee. Realize that not everything you delegate can take precedence. This does nothing except frustrate. Do you really want him to drop everything and take on this project? Specific deadlines are a must. Avoid indefinite deadlines such as 'whenever you can get it', or 'by sometime next month'. Be sure to establish some kind of reporting process so that you can keep abreast of the subordinate's progress. Together, schedule the necessary checkpoint meetings. Doing this together gives the employee a chance to consider other workload demands on his time. For a simple task, one or two checkpoints may be sufficient; more complex tasks require regular meetings with specific agendas and mini-deadlines. Make sure the subordinate knows that all checkpoints and the final deadline are firm.

Grant the necessary authority

Whenever you assign work, it's vital to give the person power to act, to exercise initiative. Make sure that all persons affected by the delegation know that you've delegated authority to this person. If appropriate, introduce your subordinate to everyone involved in completing the task: supervisors, colleagues, support staff. Make it clear that your subordinate now has the authority to do the job and that you expect him or her to work through any problems that arise.

Assign responsibility/accountability

Always delegate an entire task. This heightens your subordinate's interest and sense of accomplishment. Granting authority makes your delegation more effective. Make the delegation stick. Emphasize your confidence in the employee at every opportunity, even if you have to force yourself. Don't show fake confidence, but do compliment the employee throughout the task when something is done well. Your support often means more than your specific advice. Review work only at scheduled checkpoints or when the job is finished.

Stressing the delegatee's accountability for the task accomplishes two things. First, it makes clear that the ball is in his court. He carries the burden for results. Of course, you're still ultimately responsible to your boss, but your subordinate is accountable to you. There must be no room for confusion about that. Second, accountability contributes to the person's sense of independence. It provides positive pressure and motivation. Emphasize that the delegatee is free to make decisions relevant to this task. To some subordinates, this may be a new experience. Make it clear that, within certain limits, what they decide in this matter goes.

Obtain acceptance of the project

Always elicit from your subordinate a clear and definite acceptance of the delegated task and the intended results. You want more than murmured approval or tacit acceptance. You need an outright statement that the person agrees to the goals and the deadline. Perhaps you should both sign your copies of the revised statement of goals and timescales. Also consider the handshake as a final acceptance of the project. Although we often forget about the handshake, the axiom still applies that a person's handshake is their word. This is entirely appropriate as a way of cementing the project.

Delegation is a definite process. As you develop your delegation skills through practice, be careful constantly to review these specific steps; they will eventually become second nature to you. However, the operative word here is practice – *practice, practice, practice*!

Here are some useful tools for the delegation process:

- tickler files – allow you to keep track of the dates on which assignments are due;

- desk and calendar planners – allow long-range planning and easy-to-follow agendas at a glance;

- daily, weekly and monthly agendas – keep your mind moving and allow you to keep track of your work flow;

- employee agendas – allow you to keep track of their work flow and to see, at a glance, if assignments are being completed;

- weekly staff meetings (with an agenda) – help you to discover any operating problems and check up on assigned tasks.

11

Letting go

If you ride a horse, sit close and tight. If you ride a man, sit easy and light.
Benjamin Franklin

Once you've delegated a task, let your delegatee have an honest, fair try at it. Don't meddle! Let them do it their way, even if it's not 'the right way'. Avoid trespassing on authority once it is given. Make sure the jobs you give your people are whole and important – and that you really give them the jobs. Delegation, like a kite, will fail to fly unless you give enough slack to soar. If you take back or short-circuit assignments, your interfering will only frustrate subordinates.

Helping a delegatee grow and improve through devising a series of successes does not mean seeking to avoid all mistakes when you delegate. Not every delegated task gets done or is done correctly. In fact, mistakes are an essential part of learning through experience. Mistakes aptly illustrate what not to do. And the person who has learned what not to do is wiser than the person who has never been allowed to venture far enough to make an error. Of course you don't want your subordinates to make so many errors that they are intimidated by them, so you should limit the chances for mistakes.

Remember a subordinate's failure may simply mean that you're delegating without following through. Your controls may have failed. If a person doesn't complete a task, return to goal setting. This is a training problem. If a person won't do something, you, as manager, need to tackle that problem. Proper systems for monitoring subordinates' work will prevent large-scale failures.

Once subordinates recognize that they have made errors, don't rub it in. Emphasize the positive. Find something they did right and compliment them. Then correct and demonstrate how their errors might have been avoided. Remember, only reprimand someone when the person can do better. When you leave your people after a reprimand, you want them to think about what they did wrong, not the way you treated them. Allow yourself only a few minutes to share your feelings. When it's over – it's over. Don't keep haranguing the person for the same mistake. In the same way, focus on efforts, not circumstances. When you end a reprimand with praise, people think about their behaviour, not yours. People can take only a limited amount of criticism at any one time. When they reach their limit, they become defensive, begin to reject the validity of the criticism and tune out altogether. So, when a subordinate really bungles an assignment, try to help him to iron out the wrinkles piecemeal rather than giving them all the bad news at once. And mix in a little praise with the bitter medicine to help the person swallow it.

Meddle no; monitor yes. Never forget: what you were responsible for before delegating, you are responsible for after delegating. Follow-up is essential to the delegation process. Finding the right degree of follow-up – to guide without interfering, to protect against disaster without pampering, to advise without diminishing accountability – is a complicated, subtle aspect of the art of delegation. To avoid letting a delegated task get away from you, set up automatic system checks so you'll get regular flash reports (weekly, daily or monthly – whatever is appropriate) on how it's coming along. As a result of these reports, you may be able to readjust the project based on new data. Or you may find the project in chaos, at which time you can get involved and apply some first aid. The best way to get a surprise in business is to delegate a project and forget about it till it's done. And in business, surprises are rarely good.

12

Responsibility

Everybody threw the blame on me. I have noticed that they nearly always do. I suppose it is because they think I shall be able to bear it best.
Winston Churchill

It is a myth that, by delegating, the manager can avoid responsibility and consequent worry. Managers who delegate need to have broad shoulders. They must be prepared to accept the complete responsibility if their delegation is less than successful. Assigning duties to others is not a passport to freedom from worry and responsibility. That escape-hatch is abdication, not delegation. Ultimate accountability rests permanently with the person at the top. Problems inherent in delegation are tied directly to the emotions of those involved. The lunch-snatcher and the briefcase-lugger who refuse to delegate suffer from a feeling of loss of control whenever they delegate. The delegator must think through how they will act if they discover that things have not gone as they should. They must realize that the actions taken by others may not be the same as those they would have taken. Accommodation of differences is perhaps the hardest part of learning to delegate. While it is easy to accept the idea that people are not the same, it is much harder to accept its application. There can be immense variations not only in the quality and quantity of work performed, but also in the ways the work is performed. The manager must be prepared to accept and live with his subordinates' methods and decisions. It's a tall order, but you cannot reap the benefits of delegation unless you are willing to accept the risks. Although you don't have to agree with your subordinates at all times, you must never leave them without support. Your people depend on you. Failure to support them when they need you will always undermine their trust in your leadership.

Courage is required to risk delegating. It has been said that executives typically have a temperamental aversion to taking chances. Delegation is a calculated risk, and we must expect that over time the gains will offset the losses. We must see the risk and adjust emotionally as well as intellectually in order to delegate effectively. What you were responsible for before delegating you are responsible for after delegating.

Give your subordinates credit for their successes with delegated tasks. But if they fail, take the blame yourself. Sound unfair? It is. But it's an important and necessary rule to follow when delegating. The key word is trust. To build a team, your people must be able to trust that you will always be there for them.

Why should your subordinates knock themselves out if you are going to bask in the glory of their work? Teamwork is essential, but the coach has to credit his players who perform, not polish his own star. The delegator does need broad shoulders, but also a small enough ego to leave the spotlight solely for the person who did the work.

13

The importance of spot checking delegation: an example

No man can see all with his own eyes or do all with his own hands. Whoever is engaged in multiplicity of business must transact much by substitution and leave some things to hazard, and he who attempts to do all will waste his life doing little.
Samuel Johnson

Wayne, the production manager of Smith Shelving, believes in delegating authority just as the management books tell him to. A very busy man, he wants desperately to unload some responsibility on his employees. This is what happened on the Lacey job, a job that had to be redone because John messed up the dimensions. Lacey, the contractor, had been furious at the delay and had threatened to stop doing business with Smith unless the job was redone within weeks. Wayne knew it was a tight schedule when he promised Mike, the company's sales director, that he would meet it. Wayne immediately wrote out the new work order, checked all the dimensions and personally dropped it into Carl's work-order box with a big note written in red, stating 'Carl, get to this right away. Highest priority!' How was he to know that Carl, his best carpenter, would catch a cold and be out for a week? Two weeks later, when Wayne was on his way to a project status meeting, he saw Carl and asked how the job was going. When Carl said, 'Which job?', Wayne sensed trouble. When he explained which job, Carl answered, 'Oh, that one. I didn't see your note until four days ago when I returned from sick leave. By the way, there are a few things I wanted to get straight before I start. You know we're out of those special cedar panels? How many do you want me to order? They take a week or two to deliver.' Wayne was angry with Carl and he berated him on the shopfloor in front of others, which he knew he shouldn't do. The pity was that Wayne was more angry at himself for not having the good sense to check the job's progress sooner.

That's what happens to people who hope for the best and don't get it. Progress reports are essential in delegation. The degree and kind of spot checks will vary with the jobs. Obviously, a small delegation can be handled with an oral report at a predetermined time and date. However, handling a major order for an irritated customer with a customer-imposed deadline may require daily progress reports. Preparation of a major funding request that you will be working on for weeks may need to have three or four written reports to follow up on progress of the project.

There are a variety of means that you can use to monitor the delegation: informal meetings, memos, formal reports, flow charts, checklists, calendars, etc. The key factor here is that you must have a schedule. You must control to avoid disaster. The responsibility rests with you.

14

Making it stick: handling reverse delegation

I like the sayers of 'No' better than the sayers of 'Yes'.
Ralph Waldo Emerson

Once you've assigned a task to a subordinate, don't allow yourself to be manipulated into relieving the subordinate of the responsibility for taking the next step. This can happen in the blink of an eye. If you allow yourself to be buttonholed in a corridor or the lift, the talk may be, 'We've got a problem'. The 'we' implies that the subordinate believes that you and he are sharing the responsibility for the next step. Say the wrong thing – such as 'Let me get back to you' –

and the responsibility is right back on your shoulders.

Handle this kind of situation by making the next move the subordinate's. For example, say to the subordinate, 'You're right. There is a problem there. Give me a call tomorrow and tell me how it should be handled. What are the alternatives?' Avoid using the word 'we' in your response.

Remember, the best manager isn't always the one with the best answers, but the one with the best questions. Each time you hand out an assigned task, your subordinate can act in one of five different ways:

1. do nothing until told;

2. ask what to do;

3. recommend action, then take it;

4. act, then advise you immediately;

5. act, then report to you in a routine manner.

The astute delegator will not permit numbers one and two to occur. Do so, and you'll become so occupied with what subordinates are doing that your time will become subordinate-imposed time. You won't be able to focus on what's important to you. You're no longer in control.

Always remember that time spent in doing things for your subordinate is always subordinate-imposed time, says William Oncken, Jr., author of *Managing Management Time*. Time spent doing things with them is always discretionary time. 'Whenever possible do things with them rather than for them'.

There are a variety of reasons for the phenomenon of reverse delegation:

● *Your subordinate wishes to avoid risk.*   It is easier to ask the boss than for your subordinate to decide for themself. Asking the boss is a way of sharing the responsibility.

● *Your subordinate is afraid of criticism.*   Be careful to establish a sound system of offering constructive criticism in private.

● *Your subordinate lacks confidence.*   Be patient and delegate anyway. Without experience, no one will develop confidence.

● *Your subordinate lacks the necessary information and resources.*   No responsibility should be delegated without the requisite tools and authority.

● *The boss wants to be needed.*   The manager who is insecure with delegating authority to others is easily discernible. Employees soon sense whether the manager truly wants them to act on their own. If not, they will cater to the boss's need for omnipotence.

Often, people will go back to the boss with questions, not because they truly have questions but because they want reassurance or praise for their efforts. Remember to catch them doing something right. Constantly compliment and reinforce when small parts of tasks are done well. Training your staff to handle delegationed work is a long and sometimes arduous road. Be patient, constantly review the process and keep your guard up against reverse delegation.

15

Handling projects delegated to you

Heaven ne'er helps the men who will not act.
Sophocles

Now that you have given thought to your delegation consciousness, what about your role as the delegatee? The chances are that, in addition to being the delegator, you are also on occasion the delegatee. What happens when your manager delegates a project to you? How do you handle it?

The first thing to ask when you receive a delegation is, 'Why me?' What was it about me that prompted the boss to delegate this job to me? Is this something that I am particularly adept at? Is this something that I really need to learn more about to be better at my job? What will my performance on this task tell my boss about my abilities? Once you determine why, it is easier to chart your activities to accomplish the task.

Be sure that you have your own agenda for the delegation meeting.

- Do you understand what the desired results are?

- Do you understand specifically how the results will be measured?

- Do you agree with the schedule for the work? Can you handle this project and your other obligations at the same time?

- Do you have the authority, resources and people to do the work?

Keep in mind the professional advantages you'll gain by accepting the delegation challenge:

- Successful delegation will make your boss look good. Put in the extra effort to make the delegation work. This will increase the likelihood of future delegations being made to you.

- Successful delegation will give you invaluable professional experience. Obviously, the praise you receive for successfully handling a delegation will bring your name to mind for future projects. If you feel that you are lacking experience in a specific area of operation, explain the mutual advantages of delegation to your manager.

Remember, a prime motivator to your employees is your demonstration of the correct delegation behaviour for them. Most of the principles that apply here are the flip side of all the concepts previously discussed in motivating your employees to accept the challenge of delegation.

A note regarding delegations directed to you. If your boss is a skilled delegator, you are lucky. If his or her delegation consciousness could use some improvement, this is a challenge for you. Take the opportunities that arise to discuss the advantages of their delegating projects to you. Be careful here: You must not make your boss think that you are moving in on his or her territory. Be aware of your boss's sensitivities and insecurities. You must subtly point out the advantages of delegation in increasing your boss's productivity. No manager wants to delegate their way to a demotion. In order to reinforce your manager's sense of security, remember to emphasize the following.

- Delegation produces increased results/productivity.

- Delegation increases efficiency.

- Delegation requires checks and balances for control.

- Delegation – properly executed – makes everyone look good.

Index